KU-169-140

PUBLISHING

Kaplan Publishing are constantly finding new ways to make a difference to your studies and our exciting online resources really do offer something different to AAT students looking for exam success.

THIS BRAND NEW KAPLAN AAT REVISION KIT COMES WITH FREE EN-gage ONLINE RESOURCES TO ENSURE YOUR ARE PREPARED FOR YOUR ASSESSMENT

Having purchased this Kaplan Revision Kit, you have access to the following online study materials:

- An online Mock Exam
- Extra practice questions to test your understanding

How to access your online resources

- **Kaplan Financial students** will already have a Kaplan EN-gage account and these extra resources will be available to you online. You do not need to register again, as this process was completed when you enrolled. If you are having problems accessing online materials, please ask your course administrator.
- **If you purchased through Kaplan Flexible Learning or via the Kaplan Publishing website** you will automatically receive an e-mail invitation to Kaplan EN-gage online. Please register your details using this e-mail to gain access to your content. If you do not receive the e-mail or book content, please contact Kaplan Flexible Learning.
- **If you are already a registered Kaplan EN-gage user** go to www.EN-gage.co.uk and log in. Select the 'add a book' feature and enter the ISBN number of this book and the unique pass key at the bottom of this card. Then click 'finished' or 'add another book'. You may add as many books as you have purchased from this screen.
- **If you are a new Kaplan EN-gage user** register at www.EN-gage.co.uk and click on the link contained in the e-mail we sent you to activate your account. Then select the 'add a book' feature, enter the ISBN number of this book and the unique pass key at the bottom of this card. Then click 'finished' or 'add another book'.

Your Code and Information

This code can only be used once for the registration of one book online. This registration will expire when the final sittings for the examinations covered by this book have taken place. Please allow one hour from the time you submitted your book details for us to process your request.

iywA-aCRo-RTyh-Slti

Please be aware that this code is case-sensitive and you will need to include the dashes within the passcode, but not when entering the ISBN. For further technical support, please visit www.EN-gage.co.uk

Level 3

Costs and Revenues

REVISION KIT

British Library Cataloguing-in-Publication Data

A catalogue record for this book is available from the British Library.

Published by:

Kaplan Publishing UK

Unit 2 The Business Centre

Molly Millar's Lane

Wokingham

Berkshire

RG41 2QZ

ISBN: 978-0-85732-237-1

© Kaplan Financial Limited, 2010

Printed in Great Britain by WM Print, Walsall.

CONTENTS

Features in this exam kit

In addition to providing a wide ranging bank of real exam style questions, we have also included in this kit:

- Paper specific information and advice on exam technique.
- Our recommended approach to make your revision for this particular subject as effective as possible.

You will find a wealth of other resources to help you with your studies on the AAT website:

www.aat.org.uk/

INDEX TO QUESTIONS AND ANSWERS

EXAM TECHNIQUE

- **Do not skip any of the material** in the syllabus.
- **Read each question** *very* carefully.
- **Double-check your answer** before committing yourself to it.
- Answer **every** question – if you do not know an answer to a multiple choice question or true/false question, you don't lose anything by guessing. Think carefully before you **guess.**
- If you are answering a multiple-choice question, **eliminate first those answers that you know are wrong.** Then choose the most appropriate answer from those that are left.
- **Don't panic** if you realise you've answered a question incorrectly. Getting one question wrong will not mean the difference between passing and failing

Computer-based exams – tips

- Do not attempt a CBA until you have **completed all study material** relating to it.
- On the AAT website there is a CBA demonstration. It is **ESSENTIAL** that you attempt this before your real CBA. You will become familiar with how to move around the CBA screens and the way that questions are formatted, increasing your confidence and speed in the actual exam.
- Be sure you understand how to use the **software** before you start the exam. If in doubt, ask the assessment centre staff to explain it to you.
- Questions are **displayed on the screen** and answers are entered using keyboard and mouse. At the end of the exam, you are given a certificate showing the result you have achieved.
- In addition to the traditional multiple-choice question type, CBAs will also contain **other types of questions**, such as number entry questions, drag and drop, true/false, pick lists or drop down menus or hybrids of these.
- You need to be sure you **know how to answer questions** of this type before you sit the exam, through practice.

PAPER SPECIFIC INFORMATION

THE EXAM

FORMAT OF THE ASSESSMENT

The exam is divided into two sections:

Section 1 is concerned with the knowledge and techniques required for dealing with direct costs and revenues, and with the treatment of overhead costs in the short term. This includes calculation and/or explanations relating to inventory control, cost accounting journals, direct labour cost, allocation and apportionment of indirect costs to responsibility centres and overhead absorption rates including under and over absorptions.

Section 2 is concerned with the knowledge and techniques required for decision-making, using both short term and long term estimates of costs and revenues. This includes calculations and/or explanations relating to changes in unit costs/profit as activity levels change and profit/loss by product, break-even (CVP) analysis, limiting factor decision making, process costing, reconciling budget and actual costs and revenues by means of flexible or fixed budgets and capital investment appraisal

Learning objectives

On completion of these units the learner will be able to:

*   demonstrate an understanding of the role of costing within the organisation

*   advise on the most appropriate costing methods to use within an organisation

*   understand the principles of using costing as a decision making tool

*   record and analyse information relating to costs

*   apportion costs according to organisational requirements

*   correctly identify any significant deviations and report these to management

Time allowed

1 ½ hours

PASS MARK

The pass mark for all AAT CBAs is 70%.

 Always keep your eye on the clock and make sure you attempt all questions!

DETAILED SYLLABUS

The detailed syllabus and study guide written by the AAT can be found at:

www.aat.org.uk/

KAPLAN'S RECOMMENDED REVISION APPROACH

QUESTION PRACTICE IS THE KEY TO SUCCESS

Success in professional examinations relies upon you acquiring a firm grasp of the required knowledge at the tuition phase. In order to be able to do the questions, knowledge is essential.

However, the difference between success and failure often hinges on your exam technique on the day and making the most of the revision phase of your studies.

The **Kaplan textbook** is the starting point, designed to provide the underpinning knowledge to tackle all questions. However, in the revision phase, poring over text books is not the answer.

The **Kaplan workbook** helps you consolidate your knowledge and understanding and is a useful tool to check whether you can remember key topic areas.

Kaplan pocket notes are designed to help you quickly revise a topic area, however you then need to practise questions. There is a need to progress to exam style questions as soon as possible, and to tie your exam technique and technical knowledge together.

The importance of question practice cannot be over-emphasised.

The recommended approach below is designed by expert tutors in the field, in conjunction with their knowledge of the examiner and the specimen assessment.

You need to practise as many questions as possible in the time you have left.

OUR AIM

Our aim is to get you to the stage where you can attempt exam questions confidently, to time, in a closed book environment, with no supplementary help (i.e. to simulate the real examination experience).

Practising your exam technique is also vitally important for you to assess your progress and identify areas of weakness that may need more attention in the final run up to the examination.

In order to achieve this we recognise that initially you may feel the need to practice some questions with open book help.

Good exam technique is vital.

KAPLAN PUBLISHING

THE KAPLAN CRS REVISION PLAN

Stage 1: Assess areas of strengths and weaknesses

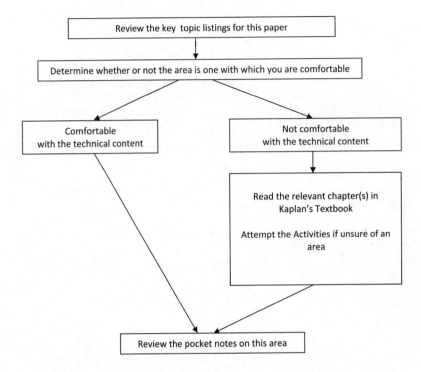

Stage 2: Practise questions

Follow the order of revision of topics as presented in this kit and attempt the questions in the order suggested.

Try to avoid referring to text books and notes and the model answer until you have completed your attempt.

Review your attempt with the model answer and assess how much of the answer you achieved.

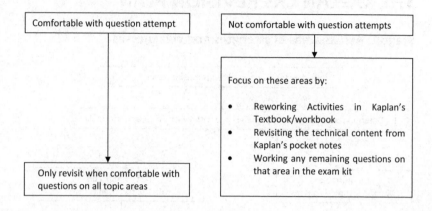

Comfortable with question attempt	Not comfortable with question attempts

Focus on these areas by:

- Reworking Activities in Kaplan's Textbook/workbook
- Revisiting the technical content from Kaplan's pocket notes
- Working any remaining questions on that area in the exam kit

Only revisit when comfortable with questions on all topic areas

Stage 3: Final pre-exam revision

We recommend that you **attempt at least one two hour mock examination** containing a set of previously unseen exam standard questions.

Attempt the mock CBA online in timed, closed book conditions to simulate the real exam experience

Section 1

PRACTICE QUESTIONS

PRINCIPLES OF COST ACCOUNTING

Cost Behaviours

1   Sarloue Ltd has prepared a forecast for the next quarter for one of its engineered components, GG57. The forecast is based on selling and producing 1,000,000 units.

One of the customers of Sarloue Ltd has indicated that it may be significantly increasing its order level for component GG57 for the next quarter and it appears that activity levels of 1,500,000 and 2,000,000 units are feasible.

The semi-variable costs should be calculated using the high-low method. If 2,000,000 units are sold the total semi-variable cost will be £60,000,000 and there is a constant unit variable cost up to this volume.

Complete the table below and calculate the estimated profit per batch of GG57 at the different activity levels.

Units produced and sold	1,000,000	1,500,000	2,000,000
	£000	£000	£000
Sales revenue	469,750		
Variable costs:			
• Direct materials	65,000		
• Direct labour	97,500		
• Overheads	78,500		
Semi-variable costs:	40,000		
• Variable element			
• Fixed element			
Total cost	281,000		
Total profit	188,750		
Profit per unit (£)	£188,750		

2   Cartcyle Ltd has prepared a forecast for the next quarter for one of its wooden products, DR43. This component is produced in batches and the forecast is based on selling and producing 2,160 batches.

One of the customers of Cartcyle Ltd has indicated that it may be significantly increasing its order level for product DR43 for the next quarter and it appears that activity levels of 2,700 batches and 3,600 batches are feasible.

The semi-variable costs should be calculated using the high-low method. If 5,400 batches are sold the total semi-variable cost will be £13,284, and there is a constant unit variable cost up to this volume.

Complete the table below and calculate the estimated profit per batch of DR43 at the different activity levels.

Batches produced and sold	2,160	2,700	3,600
	£	£	£
Sales revenue	64,800		
Variable costs:			
• Direct materials	9,720		
• Direct labour	22,680		
• Overheads	12,960		
Semi-variable costs:	6,804		
• Variable element			
• Fixed element			
Total cost	52,164		
Total profit	12,636		
Profit per batch (to 2 decimal places)	5.85		

3   Aquarius Ltd has prepared a forecast for the next quarter for one of its small metal components, Xet. This component is produced in batches and the forecast is based on selling and producing 12,000 batches.

One of the customers of Aquarius Ltd has indicated that it may be significantly increasing its order level for component Xet for the next quarter and it appears that activity levels of 13,000 batches and 15,000 batches are feasible.

The semi-variable costs should be calculated using the high-low method. If 20,000 batches are sold the total semi-variable cost will be £27,380, and there is a constant unit variable cost up to this volume.

Complete the table below and calculate the estimated profit per batch of Xet at the different activity levels.

Batches produced and sold	12,000	13,000	15,000
	£	£	£
Sales revenue	480,000		
Variable costs:			
• Direct materials	36,000		
• Direct labour	54,000		
• Overheads	60,000		
Semi-variable costs:	19,380		
• Variable element			
• Fixed element			
Total cost	169,380		
Total profit	310,620		
Profit per batch (to 2 decimal places)	£25.89		

4   Grape Ltd has prepared a forecast for the next quarter for one of its statues – Owl. Owl is produced in batches and the forecast is based on selling and producing 800 batches.

One of the customers of Grape Ltd has indicated that it may be significantly increasing its order level for Owl for the next quarter and it appears that activity levels of 1,200 batches and 1,500 batches are feasible.

The semi-variable costs should be calculated using the high-low method. If 1,600 batches are sold the total semi-variable cost will be £4,920, and there is a constant unit variable cost up to this volume.

Complete the table below and calculate the estimated profit per batch of Owl at the different activity levels.

Batches produced and sold	800	1,200	1,500
	£	£	£
Sales revenue	24,000		
Variable costs:			
• Direct materials	3,600		
• Direct labour	8,400		
• Overheads	1,800		
Semi-variable costs:	2,520		
• Variable element			
• Fixed element			
Total cost	16,320		
Total profit	7,680		
Profit per batch (to 2 decimal places)	9.60		

5   Globe Ltd has prepared a forecast for the next quarter for Tomato fertilizer. Tomato is produced in batches and the forecast is based on selling and producing 1,800 batches.

One of the customers of Globe Ltd has indicated that it may be significantly increasing its order level for Tomato for the next quarter and it appears that activity levels of 2,700 batches is likely, with a maximum capacity of 3,380 batches.

The semi-variable costs should be calculated using the high-low method. If 3380 batches are sold the total semi-variable cost will be £6,477, and there is a constant unit variable cost up to this volume.

Complete the table below and calculate the estimated profit per batch of Tomato at the different activity levels.

Batches produced and sold	1,800	2,700	3,380
	£	£	£
Sales revenue	50,400		
Variable costs:			
• Direct materials	7.560		
• Direct labour	17,640		
• Overheads	3,780		
Semi-variable costs:	5,292		
• Variable element			
• Fixed element			
Total cost	34,272		
Total profit	16,128		
Profit per batch (to 2 decimal places)	8.96		

MATERIAL COSTS

Inventory records

6   SUPERFINE OIL

The following information is available for superfine oil S07:

- Annual demand 78,125 litres.
- Annual holding cost per litre £2
- Fixed ordering cost £5

(a)   Calculate the Economic Order Quantity (EOQ) for S07

The inventory record shown below for superfine oil S07 for the month of July has not been completed for the month.

(b)   Complete the entries in the inventory record for the two receipts on 5 and 16 July that were ordered using the EOQ method.

(c)   Complete ALL entries in the inventory record for the two issues in the month and for the closing balance at the end of July using the AVCO method of issuing inventory.
(Show the costs per litre (ltr) in £'s to 3 decimal places; and the total costs to the nearest £ - round down if 50p)

Inventory record for superfine oil S07

	Receipts			Issues			Balance	
Date	Quantity Ltrs	Cost per Ltr (£)	Total cost (£)	Quantity Ltrs	Cost per Ltr (£)	Total cost (£)	Quantity Ltrs	Total cost (£)
Balance as at 1 July							210	420
5 July		2.10						
10 July				600				
16 July		2.20						
21 July				700				

7   PLASTIC

The following information is available for plastic grade PM7:

- Annual demand 112,500 kilograms.
- Annual holding cost per kilogram £1.80
- Fixed ordering cost £3.60

(a)   Calculate the Economic Order Quantity (EOQ) for PM7

The inventory record shown below for plastic grade PM7 for the month of July has only been fully completed for the first three weeks of the month.

(b)   Complete the entries in the inventory record for the two receipts on 24 and 28 July that were ordered using the EOQ method.

(c)   Complete ALL entries in the inventory record for the two issues in the month and for the closing balance at the end of July using the FIFO method of issuing inventory.
(Show the costs per kilogram (kg) in £'s to 3 decimal places; and the total costs in whole £'s).

Inventory record for plastic grade PM7

| | Receipts | | | Issues | | | Balance | |
Date	Quantity kgs	Cost per kg (£)	Total cost (£)	Quantity kgs	Cost per kg (£)	Total cost (£)	Quantity kgs	Total cost (£)
Balance as at 22 July							198	238
24 July		2.336						
26 July				540				
28 July		2.344						
30 July				720				

8 SURESTICK GLUE

The following information is available for direct material SURESTICK GLUE:

- Fixed ordering cost £2.50
- Annual holding cost per litre £1.00
- Annual demand 30,000 litres

(a) Calculate the Economic Order Quantity (EOQ) for direct material SURESTICK GLUE (round your answer up to the nearest whole number)

The inventory record shown below for SURESTICK GLUE for the month of June has only been fully completed for the first three weeks of the month.

(b) Complete the entries in the inventory record for the two receipts on 24 and 27 June that were ordered using the EOQ method.

(c) Complete ALL entries in the inventory record for the two issues in the month and for the closing balance at the end of June using the AVCO method of issuing inventory.

(Show the costs per litre in £'s to 3 decimal places; and the total costs in whole £'s, round up to nearest whole number).

Inventory record for SURESTICK GLUE

Date	Receipts			Issues			Balance	
	Quantity litres	Cost per litre (£)	Total cost (£)	Quantity litres	Cost per litre (£)	Total cost (£)	Quantity Litres	Total cost (£)
Balance as at 23 June							65	130
24 June		2.234						
26 June				180				
27 June		2.341						
30 June				250				

9 GRAPE LTD

The following information is available for glaze used in the manufacture of statues by Grape Ltd

- Monthly demand 4,000 drums. Annual demand is 48,000 drums
- Annual holding cost per drum £8
- Fixed ordering cost £120 per order

(a) **Calculate the Economic Order Quantity (EOQ) for glaze**

The inventory record shown below for glaze for the month of January has only been fully completed for the first three weeks of the month.

(b) **Complete the entries in the inventory record for the two receipts on 25 January and 28 January that were ordered using the EOQ method.**

(c) **Complete ALL entries in the inventory record for the two issues in the month and for the closing balance at the end of December using the AVCO method of issuing inventory.**
(Show the costs per drum in £'s to 3 decimal places; and the total costs in whole £'s).

Inventory record for glaze

	Receipts			Issues			Balance	
Date	Quantity drums	Cost per drum (£)	Total cost (£)	Quantity drums	Cost per drum (£)	Total cost (£)	Quantity drums	Total cost (£)
Balance as at 22 January							1,650	1,980
25 January		1.250						
26 January				1,300				
28 January		1.302						
31 January				1,500				

10   GLOBE LTD

The following information is available for raw material chemical M2 used in the manufacture of organic fertilizers by Globe Ltd

- Quarterly demand 16,000 tonnes. Annual demand is 64,000 tonnes
- Annual holding cost per tonne £5
- Fixed ordering cost £25 per order

(a)   Calculate the Economic Order Quantity (EOQ) for chemical M2

The inventory record shown below for chemical M2 for the month of March has only been fully completed for the first three weeks of the month.

(b)   Complete the entries in the inventory record for the two receipts on 28 March and 31 March that were ordered using the EOQ method.

(c)   Complete ALL entries in the inventory record for the issues in the month and for the closing balance at the end of March using the FIFO method of issuing inventory. (Show the costs per tonne in £'s to 2 decimal places; and the total costs in whole £'s).

Inventory record for M2

Date	Receipts			Issues			Balance	
	Quantity tonnes	Cost per tonne (£)	Total cost (£)	Quantity tonnes	Cost per tonne (£)	Total cost (£)	Quantity tonnes	Total cost (£)
Balance as at 27 March							1,200	14,400
28 March		12.50						
29 March				820				
30 March		12.25						
31 March				900				

11   In a period of rising prices, which type of stock valuation shows the highest profit?

A   FIFO
B   LIFO
C   AVCO
D   None

Material Bookkeeping

12 Put the correct entries into the Journal below to record the following FOUR accounting transactions:

1. Receipt of oil into inventory paying by cheque:
2. Issue of oil from inventory to production.
3. Receipt of oil into inventory paying on credit.
4. Return of oil from inventory to supplier who had sold oil on credit.

The choices are:

A   Dr. Bank, Cr. Inventory
B   Dr. Trade Payables' Control, Cr. Inventory
C   Dr. Inventory, Cr. Bank
D   Dr. Inventory, Cr. Trade Payables' Control
E   Dr. Inventory, Cr. Production
F   Dr. Production, Cr. Inventory.

	Choice
Transaction 1	
Transaction 2	
Transaction 3	
Transaction 4	

13 Put the correct entries into the Journal below to record the following FOUR accounting transactions:

1. Receipt of plastic components into inventory paying on credit:
2. Issue of plastic components from inventory to production.
3. Receipt of plastic components into inventory paying immediately by BACS.
4. Return of plastic components from production to inventory.

The choices are:

A   Dr. Bank, Cr. Inventory
B   Dr. Trade Payables' Control, Cr. Inventory
C   Dr. Inventory, Cr. Bank
D   Dr. Inventory, Cr. Trade Payables' Control
E   Dr. Inventory, Cr. Production
F   Dr. Production, Cr. Inventory

	Choice
Transaction 1	
Transaction 2	
Transaction 3	
Transaction 4	

14 Put the correct entries into the Journal below to record the following FOUR accounting transactions:

1. Receipt of SURESTICK GLUE into inventory paying immediately by BACS.
2. Issue of SURESTICK GLUE from inventory to production.
3. Receipt of SURESTICK GLUE into inventory paying on credit.
4. Return of SURESTICK GLUE from production to inventory.

The choices are:

A   Dr. Bank, Cr. Inventory
B   Dr. Trade Payables' Control, Cr. Inventory
C   Dr. Inventory, Cr. Bank
D   Dr. Inventory, Cr. Trade Payables' Control
E   Dr. Inventory, Cr. Production
F   Dr. Production, Cr. Inventory.

	Choice
Transaction 1	
Transaction 2	
Transaction 3	
Transaction 4	

15 Put the correct entries into the Journal below to record the following FOUR accounting transactions:

1. Receipt of glaze into inventory paying on credit:
2. Issue of glaze from inventory to production.
3. Receipt of glaze into inventory paying immediately by BACS.
4. Return of glaze from production to inventory.

The choices are:

A   Dr. Bank, Cr. Inventory
B   Dr. Trade Payables' Control, Cr. Inventory
C   Dr. Inventory, Cr. Bank
D   Dr. Inventory, Cr. Trade Payables' Control
E   Dr. Inventory, Cr. Production
F   Dr. Production, Cr. Inventory.

	Choice
Transaction 1	
Transaction 2	
Transaction 3	
Transaction 4	

LABOUR COSTS

Time sheets

16 Sarloue Ltd

Below is a weekly timesheet for one of Sarloue Ltd.'s employees, who is paid as follows:

- For a basic seven and a half hour shift every day from Monday to Friday - basic pay.

- For any overtime in excess of the basic seven and a half hours, on any day from Monday to Friday - the extra hours are paid at time-and-a-half (basic pay plus an overtime premium equal to half of basic pay).

- For any hours worked on Saturday or Sunday - paid at double time (basic pay plus an overtime premium equal to basic pay).

Complete the columns headed Basic pay, Overtime premium and Total pay:

(Notes: Zero figures should be entered in cells where appropriate; Overtime pay is the premium amount paid for the extra hours worked).

Employee's weekly timesheet for week ending 21 July

Employee: A. Lander			Profit Centre: Warehouse store man			
Employee number: S007			Basic pay per hour: £8.00			
	Hours spent in work		Notes	Basic pay £	Overtime premium £	Total pay £
Monday	8		Late delivery			
Tuesday	7 ½					
Wednesday	8		Early delivery			
Thursday	8		Cleaning warehouse			
Friday	7 ½					
Saturday	4		Stock taking			
Sunday	2		Stock taking			
Total	45					

17 Cartcyle Ltd

Below is a weekly timesheet for one of Cartcyle Ltd's employees, who is paid as follows:

- For a basic six-hour shift every day from Monday to Friday - basic pay.

- For any overtime in excess of the basic six hours, on any day from Monday to Friday - the extra hours are paid at time-and-a-half (basic pay plus an overtime premium equal to half of basic pay).

- For three contracted hours each Saturday morning - basic pay.

- For any hours in excess of three hours on Saturday - the extra hours are paid at double time (basic pay plus an overtime premium equal to basic pay).

- For any hours worked on Sunday - paid at double time (basic pay plus an overtime premium equal to basic pay).

Complete the columns headed Basic pay, Overtime premium and Total pay:

(Notes: Zero figures should be entered in cells where appropriate; Overtime pay is the premium amount paid for the extra hours worked).

Employee's weekly timesheet for week ending 7 December

Employee: A.Man			Profit Centre: Wood finishing			
Employee number: C812			Basic pay per hour: £8.00			
	Hours spent on production	Hours worked on indirect work	Notes	Basic pay £	Overtime premium £	Total pay £
Monday	6	2	10am-12am cleaning of machinery			
Tuesday	2	4	9am-1pm customer care course			
Wednesday	8					
Thursday	6					
Friday	6	1	3-4pm health and safety training			
Saturday	6					
Sunday	3					
Total	37	7				

18   Aquarius Ltd

Below is a weekly timesheet for one of Aquarius Ltd's employees, who is paid as follows:

- For a basic eight-hour shift every day from Monday to Friday - basic pay.

- For any overtime in excess of the basic eight hours, on any day from Monday to Friday - the extra hours are paid at time-and-a-quarter (basic pay plus an overtime premium equal to a quarter of basic pay).

- For three contracted hours each Saturday morning - basic pay.

- For any hours in excess of three hours on Saturday - the extra hours are paid at double time (basic pay plus an overtime premium equal to basic pay).

- For any hours worked on Sunday - paid at double time (basic pay plus an overtime premium equal to basic pay).

Complete the columns headed Basic pay, Overtime premium and Total pay:

(Notes: Zero figures should be entered in cells where appropriate; Overtime pay is the premium amount paid for the extra hours worked).

Employee's weekly timesheet for week ending 7 June

Employee: J Manford			Profit Centre: Assembly			
Employee number: P380			Basic pay per hour: £10.00			
	Hours spent on production	Hours worked on indirect work	Notes	Basic pay £	Overtime premium £	Total pay £
Monday	8	2	10am-12am Customer care training			
Tuesday	4	2	9am-11am cleaning of equipment			
Wednesday	10					
Thursday	8					
Friday	8	1	3-4pm health and safety training			
Saturday	8					
Sunday	4					
Total	50	5				

19 GRAPES

Below is a weekly timesheet for one of Grape's employees, who is paid as follows:

- For a basic seven-hour shift every day from Monday to Friday - basic pay.

- For any overtime in excess of the basic seven hours, on any day from Monday to Friday - the extra hours are paid at basic pay. An overtime premium is added of 25% of basic time.

- For two contracted hours each Saturday morning - basic pay.

- For any hours in excess of two hours on Saturday - the overtime premium is paid at 75% of basic pay.

Complete the columns headed Basic pay, Overtime premium and Total pay:

(Notes: Zero figures should be entered in cells where appropriate; Overtime premium is only the extra amount paid in excess of the pay for basic hours)

Employee's weekly timesheet for week ending 31 January

Employee: Olivia Michael			Profit Centre: Moulding Department			
Employee number: P450			Basic pay per hour: £10.00			
	Hours spent on production	Hours worked on indirect work	Notes	Basic pay £	Overtime premium £	Total pay £
Monday	5	3	10am-1pm cleaning moulds			
Tuesday	3	4	9am-1pm fire training			
Wednesday	8					
Thursday	6	1				
Friday	6	1	3-4pm annual appraisal			
Saturday	3					
Total	**31**	**9**				

20   GLOBE LTD

Below is a weekly timesheet for one of Globe Ltd's employees, who is paid as follows:

- For a basic 7 -hour shift every day from Monday to Friday - basic pay.

- For any overtime in excess of the basic seven hours, on any day from Monday to Friday - the extra hours are paid at 150% (basic pay plus an overtime premium equal to half of basic pay).

- For three contracted hours each Saturday morning - basic pay.

- For any hours in excess of three hours on Saturday - the extra hours are paid at 200% (basic pay plus an overtime premium equal to basic pay).

- For any hours worked on Sunday - paid at 200% (basic pay plus an overtime premium equal to basic pay).

Complete the columns headed Basic pay, Overtime premium and Total pay:

(Notes: Zero figures should be entered in cells where appropriate; Overtime pay is the premium amount paid for the extra hours worked).

Employee's weekly timesheet for week ending 31 March

Employee: J. Webb			Profit Centre: Mixing department			
Employee number: P213			Basic pay per hour: £7			
	Hours spent on production	Hours worked on indirect work	Notes	Basic pay £	Overtime premium £	Total pay £
Monday	7					
Tuesday	7	2	Weekly Staff meeting 1 hour			
Wednesday	7	1				
Thursday	5	2	Machine set up – 2 hrs			
Friday	7					
Saturday	3					
Sunday	3		Month end Stocktaking			
Total	39	5				

Labour Bookkeeping

21 Put the correct entries into the Journal below to record the following FOUR accounting transactions:

1. Record labour costs in the cost ledger
2. Analyse direct labour costs
3. Record indirect labour costs
4. Record additional production overheads

The choices are:

A   Dr. Wages control, Cr. Bank
B   Dr. Work-in-progress, Cr. Wages control
C   Dr. Production overhead account, Cr. Wages Control
D   Dr. Production overhead control, Cr. Bank
E   Dr. Inventory, Cr. Production
F   Dr. Production, Cr. Inventory

	Choice
Transaction 1	
Transaction 2	
Transaction 3	
Transaction 4	

ACCOUNTING FOR OVERHEADS

Overhead allocation and apportionment

22   Sarloue Ltd

Sarloue Ltd's budgeted overheads for the next financial year are:

	£000	£000
Depreciation of plant and equipment		22,250
Power for production machinery		17,500
Rent and rates		23,750
Light and heat		6,250
Indirect labour costs:		
Maintenance	10,000	
Stores	12,500	
Canteen	36,000	
Total indirect labour cost		58,500

The following information is also available:

Department	Net book value of plant and equipment.	Production machinery power usage (KwH)	Floor space (square metres)	Number of employees
Production centres:				
Plastic moulding	180,000	22,500	2,000	20
Plastic extrusion	360,000	30,000	2,000	20
Support cost centres:				
Maintenance			1,000	2
Stores			3,000	2
Canteen			2,000	2
Total	540,000	52,500	10,000	24

Overheads are allocated or apportioned on the most appropriate basis. The total overheads of the support cost centres are then reapportioned to the two production centres using the direct method.

- 80% of the Maintenance cost centre's time is spent maintaining production machinery in the Plastic moulding production centre and the remainder in the Plastic extrusion production centre.

- The Stores cost centre supports the two production centres equally.

- The Canteen cost centre is reapportioned based on staff numbers.

- There is no reciprocal servicing between the three support cost centres.

Complete the overhead analysis table below:

	Basis of apportionment	Plastic moulding £000	Plastic extrusion £000	Maintenance £000	Stores £000	Canteen £000	Totals £000
Depreciation of plant and equipment							
Power for production machinery							
Rent and rates							
Light and heat							
Indirect labour							
Totals							
Reapportion Maintenance							
Reapportion Stores							
Reapportion Canteen							
Total overheads to production centres							

23 Cartcyle Ltd

Cartcyle Ltd's budgeted overheads for the next financial year are:

	£	£
Depreciation of plant and equipment		1,447,470
Power for production machinery		1,287,000
Rent and rates		188,100
Light and heat		41,580
Indirect labour costs:		
Maintenance	182,070	
Stores	64,890	
General Administration	432,180	
Total indirect labour cost		679,140

The following information is also available:

Department	Net book value of plant and equipment.	Production machinery power usage (KwH)	Floor space (square metres)	Number of employees
Production centres:				
Wood cutting	10,080,000	3,861,000		25
Wood finishing	4,320,000	2,574,000		18
Support cost centres:				
Maintenance			25,200	9
Stores			15,120	3
General Administration			10,080	12
Total	14,400,000	6,435,000	50,400	67

Overheads are allocated or apportioned on the most appropriate basis. The total overheads of the support cost centres are then reapportioned to the two production centres using the direct method.

- 70% of the Maintenance cost centre's time is spent maintaining production machinery in the Wood cutting production centre and the remainder in the Wood finishing production centre.

- The Stores cost centre makes 65% of its issues to the Wood cutting production centre, and 35% to the Wood finishing production centre.

- General Administration supports the two production centres equally.

- There is no reciprocal servicing between the three support cost centres.

Complete the overhead analysis table below:

	Basis of apportionment	Wood cutting £	Wood finishing £	Maintenance £	Stores £	General Admin £	Totals £
Depreciation of plant and equipment							
Power for production machinery							
Rent and rates							
Light and heat							
Indirect labour							
Totals							
Reapportion Maintenance							
Reapportion Stores							
Reapportion General Admin							
Total overheads to production centres							

24 Aquarious

Aquarious Ltd's budgeted overheads for the next financial year are:

	£	£
Depreciation of plant and equipment		700,000
Power for production machinery		620,000
Rent and rates		100,000
Light and heat		20,000
Indirect labour costs:		
Maintenance	102,000	
Stores	40,000	
General Administration	240,000	
Total indirect labour cost		382,000

The following information is also available:

Department	Net book value of plant and equipment.	Production machinery power usage (KwH)	Floor space (square metres)	Number of employees
Production centres:				
Assembly	4,440,000	2,210,000		10
Finishing	2,960,000	1,190,000		10
Support cost centres:				
Maintenance			12,000	6
Stores			8,000	4
General Administration			5,000	8
Total	7,400,000	3,400,000	25,000	38

Overheads are allocated or apportioned on the most appropriate basis. The total overheads of the support cost centres are then reapportioned to the two production centres using the direct method.

- 75% of the Maintenance cost centre's time is spent maintaining production machinery in the Assembly production centre and the remainder in the Finishing production centre.

- The Stores cost centre makes 50% of its issues to the Assembly production centre, and 50% to the Finishing production centre.

- General Administration supports the two production centres equally.

- There is no reciprocal servicing between the three support cost centres.

Complete the overhead analysis table below:

	Basis of apportionment	Assembly £	Finishing £	Maintenance £	Stores £	General Admin £	Totals £
Depreciation of plant and equipment							
Power for production machinery							
Rent and rates							
Light and heat							
Indirect labour							
Totals							
Reapportion Maintenance							
Reapportion Stores							
Reapportion General Admin							
Total overheads to production centres							

25 Grape LTD

Grape Ltd's budgeted overheads for the next financial year are:

	£	£
Depreciation of plant and equipment		536,100
Power for production machinery		476,600
Rent and rates		69,655
Light and heat		15,400
Indirect labour costs:		
Maintenance	67431	
Stores	24,035	
General Administration	160,070	
Total indirect labour cost		251,536

The following information is also available:

Department	Net book value of plant and equipment.	Production machinery power usage (KwH)	Floor space (square metres)	Number of employees
Production centres:				
Moulding	1,120,000	1,435,000		25
Painting	1,400,000	1,340,000		15
Support cost centres:				
Maintenance			54,000	7
Stores			18,400	3
General Administration			15,600	4
Total	2,520,000	2,775,000	88,000	54

KAPLAN PUBLISHING

Overheads are allocated or apportioned on the most appropriate basis. The total overheads of the support cost centres are then reapportioned to the two production centres using the direct method.

- 75% of the Maintenance cost centre's time is spent maintaining production machinery in the Moulding production centre and the remainder in the Painting production centre.

- The Stores cost centre makes 40% of its issues to the Moulding production centre, and 60% to the Painting production centre.

- General Administration supports the two production centres equally.

- There is no reciprocal servicing between the three support cost centres.

Complete the overhead analysis table below:

	Basis of apportionment	Moulding £	Painting £	Maintenance £	Stores £	General Admin £	Totals £
Depreciation of plant and equipment							
Power for production machinery							
Rent and rates							
Light and heat							
Indirect labour							
Totals							
Reapportion Maintenance							
Reapportion Stores							
Reapportion General Admin							
Total overheads to production centres							

26 Globe LTD

Globe Ltd's budgeted overheads for the next financial year are:

	£	£
Depreciation of plant and equipment		428,880
Power for production machinery		381,280
Rent and rates		55,724
Light and heat		12,320
Indirect labour costs:		
Maintenance	53,945	
Canteen	19,228	
General Administration	128,056	
Total indirect labour cost		201,229

The following information is also available:

Department	Net book value of plant and equipment.	Production machinery power usage (KwH)	Floor space (square metres)	Number of employees
Production centres:				
Mixing	896,000	1,148,000		20
Bagging	1,120,000	1,072,000		12
Support cost centres:				
Maintenance			43,200	6
Canteen			14,720	0
General Administration			12,480	3
Total	2,016,000	2,220,000	70,400	41

Overheads are allocated or apportioned on the most appropriate basis. The total overheads of the support cost centres are then reapportioned to the two production centres using the direct method.

- 55% of the Maintenance cost centre's time is spent maintaining production machinery in the Mixing production centre and the remainder in the Bagging production centre.

- The Canteen cost centre is apportioned between the Mixing and Bagging departments based on the employee numbers using the canteen.

- General Administration supports Mixing and Bagging in a 2:1 ratio.

- There is no reciprocal servicing between the three support cost centres.

Complete the overhead analysis table below:

	Basis of apportionment	Moulding £	Painting £	Maintenance £	Canteen £	General Admin £	Totals £
Depreciation of plant and equipment							
Power for production machinery							
Rent and rates							
Light and heat							
Indirect labour							
Totals							
Reapportion Maintenance							
Reapportion Canteen							
Reapportion General Admin							
Total overheads to production centres							

Overhead absorption

27   Sarloue Ltd's budgeted overheads and activity levels are:

	Plastic moulding	Plastic extrusion
Budgeted overheads (£000)	22,500	24,750
Budgeted direct labour hours	5,000	5,200
Budgeted machine hours	15,000	20,000

(a)   **What would the budgeted overhead absorption rate for each department, if this were set based on being heavily automated to the nearest penny?**

A   Plastic moulding £1.50/hour, Plastic extrusion £1.24/hour
B   Plastic moulding £1.50/hour, Plastic extrusion £0.62/hour
C   Plastic moulding £3/hour, Plastic extrusion £0.62/hour
D   Plastic moulding £3/hour, Plastic extrusion £1.24/hour

(b)   **What would the budgeted overhead absorption rate for each department, if this were set based on being labour intensive?**

A   Plastic moulding £4.50/hour, Plastic extrusion £2.38/hour
B   Plastic moulding £4.50/hour, Plastic extrusion £4.76/hour
C   Plastic moulding £9/hour, Plastic extrusion £4.76/hour
D   Plastic moulding £9/hour, Plastic extrusion £2.38/hour

Additional data

At the end of the quarter actual overheads incurred were found to be:

	Plastic moulding	Plastic extrusion
Actual overheads (£)	19,800	38,000

(c)   Assuming that exactly the same amount of overheads was absorbed as budgeted, what would be the under or over absorptions in the quarter?

A   Plastic moulding over absorbed £2,700, Plastic extrusion over absorbed £13,250

B   Plastic moulding over absorbed £2,700, Plastic extrusion under absorbed £13,250

C   Plastic moulding under absorbed £2,700, Plastic extrusion under absorbed £13,250

D   Plastic moulding under absorbed £2,700, Plastic extrusion over absorbed £13,250

28   Cartcyle Ltd's budgeted overheads and activity levels are:

	Wood cutting	Wood finishing
Budgeted overheads (£)	586,792	320,760
Budgeted direct labour hours	29,340	17,820
Budgeted machine hours	9,464	5,940

(a)   What would the budgeted overhead absorption rate for each department, if this were set based on their both being heavily automated?

A   Wood cutting £20/hour, Wood finishing £18/hour
B   Wood cutting £20/hour, Wood finishing £54/hour
C   Wood cutting £62/hour, Wood finishing £18/hour
D   Wood cutting £62/hour, Wood finishing £54/hour

(b)   What would the budgeted overhead absorption rate for each department, if this were set based on their both being labour intensive?

A   Wood cutting £20/hour, Wood finishing £18/hour
B   Wood cutting £20/hour, Wood finishing £54/hour
C   Wood cutting £62/hour, Wood finishing £18/hour
D   Wood cutting £62/hour, Wood finishing £54/hour

Additional data

At the end of the quarter actual overheads incurred were found to be:

	Wood cutting	Wood finishing
Actual overheads (£)	568,631	356,580

(c)   Assuming that exactly the same amount of overheads was absorbed as budgeted what were the budgeted under or over absorptions in the quarter?

A   Wood cutting over absorbed £18,161, Wood finishing over absorbed £35,820
B   Wood cutting over absorbed £18,161, Wood finishing under absorbed £35,820
C   Wood cutting under absorbed £18,161, Wood finishing under absorbed £35,820
D   Wood cutting under absorbed £18,161, Wood finishing over absorbed £35,820

29   Next quarter Aquarious Ltd's budgeted overheads and activity levels are:

	Assembly	Finishing
Budgeted overheads (£)	155,000	105,000
Budgeted direct labour hours	12,500	8,750
Budgeted machine hours	2,000	1,750

(a)   What would the budgeted overhead absorption rate for each department, if this were set based on their both being heavily automated?

A   Assembly £77.50/hour, Finishing £12/hour
B   Assembly £77.50/hour, Finishing £60/hour
C   Assembly £12.40/hour, Finishing £60/hour
D   Assembly £12.40/hour, Finishing £12/hour

(b)   What would the budgeted overhead absorption rate for each department, if this were set based on their both being labour intensive?

A   Assembly £77.50/hour, Finishing £12/hour
B   Assembly £77.50/hour, Finishing £60/hour
C   Assembly £12.40/hour, Finishing £60/hour
D   Assembly £12.40/hour, Finishing £12/hour

Additional data

At the end of the quarter actual overheads incurred were found to be:

	Assembly	Finishing
Actual overheads (£)	132,000	119,000

(c)   Assuming that exactly the same amount of overheads was absorbed as budgeted what were the budgeted under or over absorptions in the quarter?

A   Assembly over absorbed £23,000, Finishing over absorbed £14,000
B   Assembly over absorbed £23,000, Finishing under absorbed £14,000
C   Assembly under absorbed £23,000, Finishing under absorbed £14,000
D   Assembly under absorbed £23,000, Finishing over absorbed £14,000

30   Next quarter Grape Limited's budgeted overheads and activity levels are:

	Moulding Dept	Painting Dept
Budgeted overheads (£)	36,000	39,000
Budgeted direct labour hours	9,000	13,000
Budgeted machine hours	18,000	1,200

(a)   What would the budgeted overhead absorption rate for each department, if this were set based on their both being heavily automated?

A   Moulding £2/hour, Finishing £32.50/hour
B   Moulding £32.50/hour, Finishing £2/hour
C   Moulding £3/hour, Finishing £33/hour
D   Moulding £33/hour, Finishing £3/hour

(b)   What would the budgeted overhead absorption rate for each department, if this were set based on their both being labour intensive?

A   Moulding £5/hour, Finishing £4/hour
B   Moulding £4/hour, Finishing £3/hour
C   Moulding £2/hour, Finishing £4/hour
D   Moulding £4/hour, Finishing £5/hour

Additional data

At the end of the quarter actual overheads incurred were found to be:

	Moulding Dept	Painting Dept
Actual overheads (£)	37,500	42,000

(c)   Assuming that exactly the same amount of overheads was absorbed as budgeted what were the budgeted under or over absorptions in the quarter?

A   Moulding under absorbed £1,500, Painting over absorbed £3,000
B   Moulding over absorbed £1,500, Painting over absorbed £3,000
C   Moulding over absorbed £1,500, Painting under absorbed £3,000
D   Moulding under absorbed £1,500, Painting under absorbed £3,000

31   Next quarter Globe Limited's budgeted overheads and activity levels are:

	Mixing Dept	Bagging Dept
Budgeted overheads (£)	64,800	70,200
Budgeted direct labour hours	1,620	2,340
Budgeted machine hours	10,000	12,000

(a)   What would the budgeted overhead absorption rate for each department, if this were set based on their both being heavily automated?

A   Mixing £6.48/hour, Bagging £5.85/hour
B   Mixing £5.85/hour, Bagging £6.48/hour
C   Mixing £6.00/hour, Bagging £6.00/hour
D   Mixing £5.00/hour, Bagging £5.00/hour

(b)   What would the budgeted overhead absorption rate for each department, if this were set based on their both being labour intensive?

A   Mixing £35.00/hour, Bagging £40.50/hour
B   Mixing £32.50/hour, Bagging £40.00/hour
C   Mixing £40.00/hour, Bagging £30.00/hour
D   Mixing £30.00/hour, Bagging £40.00/hour

Additional data

At the end of the quarter actual overheads incurred were found to be:

	Mixing Dept	Bagging Dept
Actual overheads (£)	67,500	75,600

(c)   Assuming that exactly the same amount of overheads was absorbed as budgeted what were the budgeted under or over absorptions in the quarter?

A   Mixing under absorbed £1,500, Bagging over absorbed £3,000
B   Mixing under absorbed £2,700, Bagging under absorbed £5,400
C   Mixing over absorbed £2,700, Bagging over absorbed £5,400
D   Mixing under absorbed £1,500, Bagging under absorbed £3,000

PROCESS COSTING

Losses

32   The Plastic extrusion department of Sarloue Ltd uses process costing for some of its products.

The process account for January for one particular process has been partly completed but the following information is also relevant:

Two employees worked on this process during January. Each employee worked 37.5 hours per week for 4 weeks and was paid £8 per hour.

Overheads are absorbed on the basis of £12.50 per labour hour.

Sarloue Ltd expects a normal loss of 10% during this process, which it then sells for scrap at 60p per kg.

(a)   Complete the process account below for December.

Description	Kgs	Unit cost £	Total cost £	Description	Kgs	Unit cost £	Total cost £
Material A	250	6		Normal loss		0.60	
Material B	425	4		Output	675		
Material C	75	5					
Labour							
Overheads							
	750						

(b)   Identify the correct entry for each of the following in a process account.

	Debit	Credit
Abnormal loss		
Abnormal gain		

33   The Wood finishing department of Cartcyle Ltd uses process costing for some of its products.

The process account for July for one particular process has been partly completed but the following information is also relevant:

Two employees worked on this process during December. Each employee worked 40 hours per week for 4 weeks and was paid £18 per hour.

Overheads are absorbed on the basis of £28.80 per labour hour.

Cartcyle Ltd expects a normal loss of 5% during this process, which it then sells for scrap at £1.08 per kg.

Complete the process account below for July.

Description	Kgs	Unit cost £	Total cost £	Description	Kgs	Unit cost £	Total cost £
Material TR10	1,080	2.16		Normal loss		1.08	
Material DG41	720	2.70		Output	2,300		
Material IG11	720	1.10					
Labour							
Overheads							

34   The metal finishing department of Aquarius Ltd uses process costing for some of its products.

The process account for December for one particular process has been partly completed but the following information is also relevant:

Two employees worked on this process during December. Each employee worked 40 hours per week for 4 weeks and was paid £8 per hour.

Overheads are absorbed on the basis of £12 per labour hour.

Aquarius Ltd expects a normal loss of 2% during this process, which it then sells for scrap at 50p per kg.

(a)   Complete the process account, the normal loss and the abnormal loss/gain accounts below for December.

Process account

Description	Kgs	Unit cost £	Total cost £	Description	Kgs	Unit cost £	Total cost £
Material CBB	700	1.30		Normal loss		0.50	
Material BSS	500	1.12		Output	1,600		
Material SMA	500	0.72					
Labour							
Overheads							

Normal loss account

Description	Kgs	Unit cost £	Total cost £	Description	Kgs	Unit cost £	Total cost £

Abnormal loss/gain account

Description	Kgs	Unit cost £	Total cost £	Description	Kgs	Unit cost £	Total cost £

35 The Glazing department of Grape Ltd uses process costing for glazing finished statues.

The process account for January for one particular process has been partly completed but the following information is also relevant:

Four employees worked on this process during January. Each employee worked 30 hours per week for 4 weeks and was paid £12 per hour.

Overheads are absorbed on the basis of £8 per labour hour.

Grape Ltd expects a normal loss of 10% during this process, which it then sells for scrap at £5 per kg.

(a) Complete the process account below for January.

Description	Units	Unit cost £	Total cost £		Description	Units	Unit cost £	Total cost £
Input - Statues	300	11.25	3,375		Normal loss		5.00	
Materials - Glaze			500		Output	290		
Labour								
Overheads								

36 The finishing department of Globe Ltd uses process costing for manufacturing liquid fertilizers.

The process account for March for one particular process has been partly completed but the following information is also relevant:

Three employees worked on this process during March. Each employee worked 32 hours per week for 4 weeks and was paid £10 per hour.

Overheads are absorbed on the basis of £1.50 per labour hour.

Globe Ltd expects a normal loss of 5% during this process, which it then sells for scrap at £0.05 per kg.

(a)   Complete the process account below for March.

Description	Litres	Cost per litre £	Total cost £		Description	Litres	Cost per litre £	Total cost £
Liquid X12	500	0.02			Normal loss		0.05	
Liquid X13	200	0.04			Output	760		
Liquid X14	100	0.10						
Labour								
Overheads								

(b)   Identify the correct entry for each of the following in a process account.

	Debit	Credit
Abnormal loss		
Abnormal gain		

Equivalent units

37   Bahadra makes biscuits. Production requires several successive processes and the production details of the first process are as follows.

Volume completed in period	5000 kg
Closing work in process	600 kg
Degree of completion of closing WIP:	
Materials	100%
Labour	50%
Overheads	50%
Costs incurred in April:	
Materials	£56,000
Labour	£26,500
Overheads	£10,600

Complete the table below and the process account

Statement of EU

	Materials	Conversion
Completed		
CWIP		
TOTAL EU		
Costs		
Period Costs		
TOTAL COSTS		
Cost per EU		

Description	Kgs	Total cost £		Description	Kgs	Total cost £

38   Diamond makes graphite pencils on a production line. The details of the process in Period 2 are as follows:

OWIP   =   250 units
Costs incurred so far
                 Materials   £54,000
                 Conversion   £42,000
Degrees of completion
                 Materials   100%
                 Conversion   60%

Completed output =   3,200 units

CWIP   =   230 units
Degree of completion:
                 Materials   100%
                 Conversion   70%

Costs incurred in Period 1:
                 Materials   £135,000
                 Conversion   £99,000

Complete the process accounting using the FIFO method of valuing OWIP

Equivalent units		Material	Conversion
	OWIP to complete		
	Completed Output		
	CWIP		
	Total EU		
Costs			
	Period		
	Total cost		
Cost per EU			
(to 4 decimal places)			

Description	Units	Total cost £	Description	Units	Total cost £
OWIP					
Materials					
Conversion					

39 Silver makes key rings on a production line. The details of the process in Period 2 are as follows:

OWIP = 250 units
Costs incurred so far
      Materials   £54,000
      Conversion £42,000
Degrees of completion
      Materials   100%
      Conversion 60%

Completed output = 3,200 units

CWIP = 230 units
Degree of completion:
      Materials   100%
      Conversion 70%

Costs incurred in Period 1:
      Materials   £135,000
      Conversion £99,000

Complete the process accounting using the AVCO method of valuing OWIP

Equivalent units		Material	Conversion
	Completed Output		
	CWIP		
	Total EU		
Costs			
	OWIP		
	Period		
	Total cost		
Cost per EU			
(to 4 decimal places)			

Description	Units	Total cost £		Description	Units	Total cost £
OWIP				Completed		
Materials				CWIP		
Conversion						

BASIC VARIANCE ANALYSIS

40   Sarloue Ltd. has the following original budget and actual performance for product GG101 for the year ending 31 December.

	Budget	Actual
Volume sold	20,000	18,500
Sales revenue	40,000	38,850
Less costs:		
Direct materials	16,000	17,575
Direct labour	10,000	10,175
Overheads	2,000	1,950
Operating profit	12,000	9,150

Both direct materials and direct labour are variable costs, but the overheads are fixed

Complete the table below to show a flexed budget and the resulting variances against this budget for the year. Show the actual variance amount, for sales and each cost, in the column headed 'Variance' and indicate whether this is Favourable or Adverse by entering F or A in the final column. If neither F nor A enter 0.

	Flexed Budget	Actual	Variance	Favourable F or Adverse A
Volume sold		18,500		
Sales revenue		38,850		
Less costs:				
Direct materials		17,575		
Direct labour		10,175		
Overheads		1,950		
Operating profit		9,150		

41   Cartcyle Ltd. has the following original budget and actual performance for product CR70 for the year ending 31 July.

	Budget	Actual
Volume sold	180,000	259,200
	£000	£000
Sales revenue	3,600	6,480
Less costs:		
Direct materials	630	954
Direct labour	720	864
Overheads	1,764	2,210
Operating profit	486	2,452

Both direct materials and direct labour are variable costs, but the overheads are fixed

Complete the table below to show a flexed budget and the resulting variances against this budget for the year. Show the actual variance amount, for sales and each cost, in the column headed 'Variance' and indicate whether this is Favourable or Adverse by entering F or A in the final column. If neither F nor A enter 0.

	Flexed Budget	Actual	Variance	Favourable F or Adverse A.
Volume sold		259,200		
	£000	£000	£000	
Sales revenue		6,480		
Less costs:				
Direct materials		954		
Direct labour		864		
Overheads		2,210		
Operating profit		2,452		

42   Aquarius Ltd. has the following original budget and actual performance for product Britz for the year ending 31 December.

	Budget	Actual
Volume sold	200,000	267,000
	£000	£000
Sales revenue	1,600	2,409
Less costs:		
Direct materials	400	801
Direct labour	200	267
Overheads	600	750
Operating profit	400	591

Both direct materials and direct labour are variable costs, but the overheads are fixed

Complete the table below to show a flexed budget and the resulting variances against this budget for the year. Show the actual variance amount, for sales and each cost, in the column headed 'Variance' and indicate whether this is Favourable or Adverse by entering F or A in the final column. If neither F nor A enter 0.

	Flexed Budget	Actual	Variance	Favourable F or Adverse A.
Volume sold		267,000		
	£000	£000	£000	
Sales revenue		2,409		
Less costs:				
Direct materials		801		
Direct labour		267		
Overheads		750		
Operating profit		591		

43 Grape Ltd. has the following original budget and actual performance for product Bird Box Sets for the year ending 31 December.

	Budget	Actual
Volume sold	20,000	28,800
	£000	£000
Sales revenue	3,000	3,877
Less costs:		
Direct materials	175	212
Direct labour	875	912
Overheads	445	448
Operating profit	1,505	2,305

Both direct materials and direct labour are variable costs, but the overheads are fixed

Complete the table below to show a flexed budget and the resulting variances against this budget for the year. Show the actual variance amount, for sales and each cost, in the column headed 'Variance' and indicate whether this is Favourable or Adverse by entering F or A in the final column. If neither F nor A enter 0.

	Flexed Budget	Actual	Variance	Favourable F or Adverse A.
Volume sold		28,800		
	£000	£000	£000	
Sales revenue		3,877		
Less costs:				
Direct materials		212		
Direct labour		912		
Overheads		448		
Operating profit		2,305		

44   Globe Ltd. has the following original budget and actual performance for product Bean for the year ending 31 December.

	Budget	Actual
Volume sold (litres)	4,000	5,000
	£000	£000
Sales revenue	1,500	1,950
Less costs:		
Direct materials	36	45
Direct labour	176	182
Overheads	89	90
Operating profit	1,199	1,633

Both direct materials and direct labour are variable costs, but the overheads are fixed

Complete the table below to show a flexed budget and the resulting variances against this budget for the year. Show your answer to the nearest £1000. Show the actual variance amount, for sales and each cost, in the column headed 'Variance' and indicate whether this is Favourable or Adverse by entering F or A in the final column. If neither F nor A enter 0.

	Flexed Budget	Actual	Variance	Favourable F or Adverse A.
Volume sold	5,000	5,000		
	£000	£000	£000	
Sales revenue		1,950		
Less costs:				
Direct materials		45		
Direct labour		182		
Overheads		90		
Operating profit		1,633		

SHORT TERM DECISION MAKING

Cost Volume Profit analysis

45   Product GG99 has a selling price of £29 per unit with a total variable cost of £21 per unit. Sarloue Ltd estimates that the fixed costs per quarter associated with this product are £9,952.

(a)   Calculate the budgeted breakeven, in units, for product GG29.

```
┌──────────────────┐
│           units  │
└──────────────────┘
```

(b)   Calculate the budgeted breakeven, in £s, for product GG29.

```
┌──────────────────┐
│ £                │
└──────────────────┘
```

(c)   Complete the table below to show the budgeted margin of safety in units and the margin of safety percentage if Sarloue Ltd sells 5,000 units or 6,000 units of product GG99.

Units of GG29 sold	5,000	6,000
	£	£
Margin of safety (units)		
Margin of safety percentage		

(d)   If Sarloue Ltd wishes to make a profit of £48,000, how many units of GG99 must it sell?

(e)   If Sarloue Ltd decreases the selling price of GG99 by £1 what will be the impact on the breakeven point and the margin of safety assuming no change in the number of units sold?

A.   The breakeven point will decrease and the margin of safety will increase.
B.   The breakeven point will stay the same but the margin of safety will decrease.
C.   The breakeven point will decrease and the margin of safety will stay the same.
D.   The breakeven point will increase and the margin of safety will decrease.

46   Product MR13 has a selling price of £41.40 per unit with a total variable cost of £27 per unit. Cartcyle Ltd estimates that the fixed costs per quarter associated with this product are £64,800.

(a)   Calculate the budgeted breakeven point, in units, for product MR13.

units

(b)   Calculate the budgeted breakeven revenue, in £s, for product MR13.

£

(c)   Complete the table below to show the budgeted margin of safety in units and the margin of safety percentage if Cartcyle Ltd sells 9,000 units or 10,800 units of product MR13.

Units of MR13 sold	9,000	10,800
	£	£
Margin of safety (units)		
Margin of safety percentage		

(d)   If Cartcyle Ltd wishes to make a profit of £36,000, how many units of MR13 must it sell?

	units

(e)   If Cartcyle Ltd increases the selling price of MR13 by £1.80 what will be the impact on the breakeven point and the margin of safety assuming no change in the number of units sold?

A.   The breakeven point will decrease and the margin of safety will increase.

B.   The breakeven point will stay the same but the margin of safety will decrease.

C.   The breakeven point will decrease and the margin of safety will stay the same.

D.   The breakeven point will increase and the margin of safety will decrease.

47   Product component CoralZ has a selling price of £19 per unit with a total variable cost of £12 per unit. Aquarius Ltd estimates that the fixed costs per quarter associated with this product are £17,000.

(a)   Calculate the budgeted breakeven, in units, for product CORALZ.

	units

(b)   Calculate the budgeted breakeven, in £s, for product CORALZ.

£	

(c)   Complete the table below to show the budgeted margin of safety in units and the margin of safety percentage if Aquarius Ltd sells 4,000 units or 5,000 units of product CORALZ.

Units of CORALZ sold	4,000	5,000
	£	£
Margin of safety (units)		
Margin of safety percentage		

(d)   If Aquarius Ltd wishes to make a profit of £25,000, how many units of CORALZ must it sell?

units

(e)   If Aquarius Ltd increases the selling price of CORALZ by £2 what will be the impact on the breakeven point and the margin of safety assuming no change in the number of units sold?

A.   The breakeven point will decrease and the margin of safety will stay the same.
B.   The breakeven point will decrease and the margin of safety will increase.
C.   The breakeven point will stay the same but the margin of safety will decrease.
D.   The breakeven point will increase and the margin of safety will decrease.

48   Blackbird has a selling price of £10 per unit with a total variable cost of £6 per unit. Grape Ltd estimates that the fixed costs per quarter associated with this product are £25,000.

(a)   Calculate the budgeted breakeven, in units, for Blackbird.

units

(b)   Calculate the budgeted breakeven, in £s, for product Blackbird.

£

(c)   Complete the table below to show the budgeted margin of safety in units and the margin of safety percentage if Grape Ltd sells 7,000 units or 8,000 units of Blackbird.

Units of Blackbird sold	7,000	8,000
	£	£
Margin of safety (units)		
Margin of safety percentage		

(d)   If Grape Ltd wishes to make a profit of £35,000, how many units of Blackbird must it sell?

	units

(e)   If Grape Ltd decreases the selling price of Blackbird by £0.50 what will be the impact on the breakeven point and the margin of safety assuming no change in the number of units sold?

A.   The breakeven point will decrease and the margin of safety will increase.

B.   The breakeven point will stay the same but the margin of safety will decrease.

C.   The breakeven point will decrease and the margin of safety will stay the same.

D.   The breakeven point will increase and the margin of safety will decrease.

49   Rose flower food is sold in sachets. Each sachet has a selling price of £0.10 per unit with a total variable cost of £0.04 per unit. Globe Ltd estimates that the fixed costs per quarter associated with this product are £15,000.

(a)   Calculate the budgeted breakeven, in units, for Rose.

	units

(b)   Calculate the budgeted breakeven, in £s, for product Rose.

£

(c)   Complete the table below to show the budgeted margin of safety in units and the margin of safety percentage if Globe Ltd sells 300,000 units or 400,000 units of Rose.

Units of Rose sold	300,000	400,000
	£	£
Margin of safety (units)		
Margin of safety percentage		

(d)   If Globe Ltd wishes to make a profit of £5,000, how many units of Rose must it sell?

units

(e)   If Globe Ltd increases the selling price of Rose by £0.01 what will be the impact on the breakeven point and the margin of safety assuming no change in the number of units sold?

A.   The breakeven point will increase and the margin of safety will decrease.
B.   The breakeven point will stay the same but the margin of safety will decrease.
C.   The breakeven point will decrease and the margin of safety will increase.
D.   The breakeven point will increase and the margin of safety will increase.

Limiting Factor analysis

50   Yeknom makes two products, the Apple breakfast bar and the Banana breakfast bar. The following budgeted annual sales and cost information relates to A and B:

Product	Apple bars	Banana bars
Bars made and sold	75,000	125,000
Machine hours required	30,000	20,000
Sales revenue(£)	225,000	300,000
Direct materials (£)	30,000	62,500
Direct labour (£)	18,000	35,000
Variable overheads (£)	22,500	47,500
Fixed overheads (£)	150,000	

Complete the table below (to 2 decimal places) to show the budgeted contribution per bar of Apple and bar of Banana sold, and the company's budgeted profit or loss for the year from these two products.

	Apple (£)	Banana (£)	Total (£)
Selling price per bar			
Less: variable costs per unit			
Direct materials			
Direct labour			
Variable overheads			
Contribution per unit			
Sales volume (bars)			
Total contribution			
Less: fixed costs			
Budgeted profit or loss			

Due to a machine breakdown the number of machine hours available for products Apple bars and Banana bars has now been reduced to only 35,000 during the year.

Given this limitation and your calculations, complete the table below to recommend how many bars of products Apple and Banana Yeknom should now make in order to maximise the profit from these two products for the year.

Product	Apple bars	Banana bars	Total
Contribution/unit (£)			
Machine hours/unit			
Contribution/machine hour (£)			
Product ranking			
Machine hours available			
Machine hours allocated to: Product .... Product			
Units made			
Less: fixed costs (£)			
Profit/loss made (£)			

51 Monty makes two products, the Squeaker and the Hooter. The following budgeted annual sales and cost information relates to the Squeaker and the Hooter:

Product	Squeaker	Hooter
Units made and sold	80,000	70,000
Machine hours required	40,000	17,500
Sales revenue(£)	100,000	122,500
Direct materials (£)	40,000	17,500
Direct labour (£)	20,000	35,000
Variable overheads (£)	20,000	45,500
Fixed overheads (£)	15,000	

Complete the table below (to 2 decimal places) to show the budgeted contribution per bar of Squeakers and Hooters sold, and the company's budgeted profit or loss for the year from these two products.

	Squeaker (£)	Hooter (£)	Total (£)
Selling price per bar			
Less: variable costs per unit			
Direct materials			
Direct labour			
Variable overheads			
Contribution per unit			
Sales volume (bars)			
Total contribution			
Less: fixed costs			
Budgeted profit or loss			

Due to a machine breakdown the number of machine hours available for products has now been reduced to only 50,000 during the year.

Given this limitation and your calculations, complete the table below to recommend how many units of Squeakers and Hooters Monty should now make in order to maximise the profit from these two products for the year.

Product	Squeakers	Hooters	Total
Contribution/unit (£)			
Machine hours/unit			
Contribution/machine hour (£)			
Product ranking			
Machine hours available			
Machine hours allocated to: Product .... Product			
Units made			
Less: fixed costs (£)			
Profit/loss made (£)			

LONG TERM DECISION MAKING

NPV and payback

52   One of the extrusion machines in the Plastic extrusion department is nearing the end of its useful life and Broadsword Ltd is considering purchasing a replacement machine.

Estimates have been made for the initial capital cost, sales income and operating costs of the replacement machine, which is expected to have a useful life of three years:

	Year 0 £000	Year 1 £000	Year 2 £000	Year 3 £000
Capital expenditure	450			
Other cash flows:				
Sales income		600	650	750
Operating costs		420	480	530

The company appraises capital investment projects using a 15% cost of capital.

(a) **Complete the table below and calculate the net present value of the proposed replacement machine (to the nearest £000).**

	Year 0 £000	Year 1 £000	Year 2 £000	Year 3 £000
Capital expenditure				
Sales income				
Operating costs				
Net cash flows				
PV factors	1.0000	0.8696	0.7561	0.6575
Discounted cash flows				
Net present value				

The net present value is *positive/negative**
**delete as appropriate*

(b) **Calculate the payback of the proposed replacement machine to the nearest whole month.**

The payback period is ---------- Year(s) and ------------ Months

53 One of the finishing machines in the Wood finishing department is nearing the end of its useful life and Cartcyle Ltd is considering purchasing a replacement machine.

Estimates have been made for the initial capital cost, sales income and operating costs of the replacement machine, which is expected to have a useful life of three years:

	Year 0 £000	Year 1 £000	Year 2 £000	Year 3 £000
Capital expenditure	1,620			
Other cash flows:				
Sales income		756	1,008	1,440
Operating costs		216	270	342

The company appraises capital investment projects using a 15% cost of capital.

(a) **Complete the table below and calculate the net present value of the proposed replacement machine (to the nearest £000).**

	Year 0 £000	Year 1 £000	Year 2 £000	Year 3 £000
Capital expenditure				
Sales income				
Operating costs				
Net cash flows				
PV factors	1.0000	0.8696	0.7561	0.6575
Discounted cash flows				
Net present value				

The net present value is *of positive/negative**
*delete as appropriate

(b) **Calculate the payback of the proposed replacement machine to the nearest whole month.**

The payback period is ---------- Year(s) and ------------ Months

54 One of the finishing machines in the metal finishing department is nearing the end of its useful life and Aquarius Ltd is considering purchasing a replacement machine.

Estimates have been made for the initial capital cost, sales income and operating costs of the replacement machine, which is expected to have a useful life of four years:

	Year 0 £000	Year 1 £000	Year 2 £000	Year 3 £000
Capital expenditure	1,200			
Other cash flows:				
Sales income		530	570	700
Operating costs		140	160	190

The company appraises capital investment projects using a 15% cost of capital.

(a) Complete the table below and calculate the net present value of the proposed replacement machine (to the nearest £000).

	Year 0 £000	Year 1 £000	Year 2 £000	Year 3 £000
Capital expenditure				
Sales income				
Operating costs				
Net cash flows				
PV factors	1.0000	0.8696	0.7561	0.6575
Discounted cash flows				
Net present value				

The net present value is *positive/negative**
delete as appropriate

(b) Net cash inflow in year 4 is £530,000, calculate the payback of the proposed replacement machine to the nearest whole month.

The payback period is   ---------- Year(s) and   ------------ Months

55   One of the moulding machines in the Moulding department is nearing the end of its useful life and Grape Ltd is considering purchasing a replacement machine.

Estimates have been made for the initial capital cost, sales income and operating costs of the replacement machine, which is expected to have a useful life of three years:

	Year 0 £000	Year 1 £000	Year 2 £000	Year 3 £000
Capital expenditure	500			
Other cash flows:				
Sales income		280	330	390
Operating costs		100	120	130

The company appraises capital investment projects using a 10% cost of capital.

(a) Complete the table below and calculate the net present value of the proposed replacement machine (to the nearest £000).

	Year 0 £000	Year 1 £000	Year 2 £000	Year 3 £000
Capital expenditure				
Sales income				
Operating costs				
Net cash flows				
PV factors	1.0000	0.909	0.826	0.751
Discounted cash flows				
Net present value				

The net present value is *positive/negative**
**delete as appropriate*

(b) Calculate the payback of the proposed replacement machine to the nearest whole month.

The payback period is ---------- Year(s) and ------------ Months

56 One of the machines in the Finishing department is nearing the end of its useful life and Globe Ltd is considering purchasing a replacement machine.

Estimates have been made for the initial capital cost, sales income and operating costs of the replacement machine, which is expected to have a useful life of three years:

	Year 0 £000	Year 1 £000	Year 2 £000	Year 3 £000
Capital expenditure	547			
Other cash flows:				
Sales income		290	340	400
Operating costs		120	120	120

The company appraises capital investment projects using a 10% cost of capital.

(a)   **Complete the table below and calculate the net present value of the proposed replacement machine (to the nearest £000).**

	Year 0 £000	Year 1 £000	Year 2 £000	Year 3 £000
Capital expenditure				
Sales income				
Operating costs				
Net cash flows				
PV factors	1.0000	0.909	0.826	0.751
Discounted cash flows				
Net present value				

The net present value is *positive/negative**
*delete as appropriate

(b)   **Calculate the payback of the proposed replacement machine to the nearest whole month.**

The payback period is   ---------- Year(s) and   ----------- Months

Section 2

ANSWERS TO PRACTICE QUESTIONS

PRINCIPLES OF COST ACCOUNTING

Cost Behaviours

1

Units produced and sold	1,000,000	1,500,000	2,000,000
	£000	£000	£000
Sales revenue	469,750	704,625	939,500
Variable costs:			
• Direct materials	65,000	97,500	130,000
• Direct labour	97,500	146,250	195,000
• Overheads	78,500	117,750	157,000
Semi-variable costs:	40,000		
• Variable element		30,000	40,000
• Fixed element		20,000	20,000
Total cost	281,000	411,500	542,000
Total profit	188,750	293,125	397,500
Profit per unit (£)	£188,750	£195,417	£198,750

2

Batches produced and sold	2,160	2,700	3,600
	£	£	£
Sales revenue	64,800	81,000	108,000
Variable costs:			
• Direct materials	9,720	12,150	16,200
• Direct labour	22,680	28,350	37,800
• Overheads	12,960	16,200	21,600
Semi-variable costs:	6,804		
• Variable element		5,400	7,200
• Fixed element		2,484	2,484
Total cost	52,164	64,584	85,284
Total profit	12,636	16,416	22,716
Profit per batch (to 2 decimal places)	5.85	6.08	6.31

3

Batches produced and sold	12,000	13,000	15,000
	£	£	£
Sales revenue	480,000	520,000	600,000
Variable costs:			
• Direct materials	36,000	39,000	45,000
• Direct labour	54,000	58,500	67,500
• Overheads	60,000	65,000	75,000
Semi-variable costs:	19,380		
• Variable element		13,000	15,000
• Fixed element		7,380	7,380
Total cost	169,380	182,880	209,880
Total profit	310,620	337,120	390,120
Profit per batch (to 2 decimal places)	£25.89	£25.93	£26.01

4

Batches produced and sold	800	1,200	1,500
	£	£	£
Sales revenue	24,000	36,000	45,000
Variable costs:			
• Direct materials	3,600	5,400	6,750
• Direct labour	8,400	12,600	15,750
• Overheads	1,800	2,700	3,375
Semi-variable costs:	2,520		
• Variable element		3,600	4,500
• Fixed element		120	120
Total cost	16,320	24,420	30,495
Total profit	7,680	11,580	14,505
Profit per batch (to 2 decimal places)	9.60	9.65	9.67

5

Batches produced and sold	1,800	2,700	3,380
	£	£	£
Sales revenue	50,400	75,600	94,640
Variable costs:			
• Direct materials	7.560	11,340	14,196
• Direct labour	17,640	26,460	33,124
• Overheads	3,780	5,670	7,098
Semi-variable costs:	5,292		
• Variable element		2,025	2,535
• Fixed element		3,942	3,942
Total cost	34,272	49,437	60,895
Total profit	16,128	26,163	33,745
Profit per batch (to 2 decimal places)	8.96	9.69	9.98

MATERIAL COSTS

Inventory records

6   (a) The EOQ = $\sqrt{\left(\frac{2 \times 5 \times 78,125}{2}\right)}$ = 625

(b) Inventory record card

	Receipts			Issues			Balance	
Date	Quantity Ltrs	Cost per Ltr (£)	Total cost (£)	Quantity Ltrs	Cost per Ltr (£)	Total cost (£)	Quantity Ltrs	Total cost (£)
Balance as at 1 July							210	420
24 December	625	2.10	1,312				835	1,732
26 December				600	2.074	1,244	235	488
28 December	625	2.20	1,375				860	1,863
30 December				700	2.166	1,516	160	347

7   (a) The EOQ = $\sqrt{\left(\frac{2 \times 3.60 \times 112,500}{1.80}\right)}$ = 671

(b) Inventory record card

	Receipts			Issues			Balance	
Date	Quantity kgs	Cost per kg (£)	Total cost (£)	Quantity kgs	Cost per kg (p)	Total cost (£)	Quantity kgs	Total cost (£)
Balance as at 22 June							198	238
24 June	671	2.336	1,567				869	1,805
26 June				540	198 @ 1.202 342 @ 2.336	1037	329	768
28 June	671	2.344	1,573				1,000	2,341
30 June				720	329 @ 2.336 391 @2.344	1,685	280	656

8   (a) The EOQ = $\sqrt{\left(\frac{2 \times 2.50 \times 30,000}{1.00}\right)} = 388$

(b) Inventory record card

Date	Receipts			Issues			Balance	
	Quantity litres	Cost per litre	Total cost (£)	Quantity litres	Cost per litre	Total cost (£)	Quantity Litres	Total cost (£)
Balance as at 23 June							65	130
24 June	388	2.234	867				453	997
26 June				180	2.201	397	273	600
27 June	388	2.341	909				661	1,509
30 June				250	2.283	571	411	938

9   (a) The EOQ = $\sqrt{\left(\frac{2 \times 120 \times 48,000}{8}\right)} = 1,200$

(b) Inventory record card

Date	Receipts			Issues			Balance	
	Drums	Cost per Drum (£)	Total cost (£)	Drums	Cost per drum (p)	Total cost (£)	Drums	Total cost (£)
Balance as at 22 January							1,650	1,980
25 January	1,200	1.250	1,500				2,850	3,480
26 January				1,300	1.221	1,587	1,550	1,893
28 January	1,200	1.302	1,562				2,750	3,455
31 January				1,500	1.256	1,884	1,250	1,571

10 (a) The EOQ = $\sqrt{\left(\frac{2 \times 25 \times 64,000}{5}\right)}$ = 800

(b) Inventory record card

Date	Receipts			Issues			Balance	
	Tonnes	Cost per tonne (£)	Total cost (£)	Tonnes	Cost per tonne (£)	Total cost (£)	Tonnes	Total cost (£)
Balance as at 27 March							1,200	14,400
28 March	800	12.50	10,000				2,000	24,400
29 March				820	12.00	9,840	1,180	14,560
30 March	800	12.25	9,800				1,980	24,360
31 March				900	380 @ 12 520 @12.50	11,060	1,080	13,300

11 Answer A – FIFO

Material Bookkeeping

12

	Choice
Transaction 1	(C) Dr. Inventory, Cr. Bank
Transaction 2	(F) Dr. Production, Cr. Inventory
Transaction 3	(D) Dr. Inventory, Cr. Trade Payables control
Transaction 4	(B) Dr. Trade Payables control, Cr. Inventory

13

	Choice
Transaction 1	(D) Dr. Inventory, Cr. Trade payables' Control
Transaction 2	(F) Dr. Production, Cr. Inventory
Transaction 3	(C) Dr. Inventory, Cr. Bank
Transaction 4	(E) Dr. Inventory, Cr. Production

14

	Choice
Transaction 1	(C) Dr. Inventory, Cr. Bank
Transaction 2	(F) Dr. Production, Cr. Inventory
Transaction 3	(D) Dr. Inventory, Cr. Trade payables' Control
Transaction 4	(E) Dr. Inventory, Cr. Production

15

	Choice
Transaction 1	(D) Dr. Inventory, Cr. Trade payables' Control
Transaction 2	(F) Dr. Production, Cr. Inventory
Transaction 3	(C) Dr. Inventory, Cr. Bank
Transaction 4	(E) Dr. Inventory, Cr. Production

LABOUR COSTS

Time sheets

16   Employee's weekly timesheet for week ending 21 July

Employee: A. Lander			Profit Centre: Warehouse store man			
Employee number: S007			Basic pay per hour: £8.00			
	Hours spent in work		Notes	Basic pay £	Overtime premium £	Total pay £
Monday	8		Late delivery	64	2	66
Tuesday	7½			60	0	60
Wednesday	8		Early delivery	64	2	66
Thursday	8		Cleaning warehouse	64	2	65
Friday	7 ½			60	0	60
Saturday	4		Stock taking	32	32	64
Sunday	2		Stock taking	0	32	32
Total	**37**			344	70	414

17 Employee's weekly timesheet for week ending 7 December

Employee: A. Man			Profit Centre: Wood finishing			
Employee number: C812			Basic pay per hour: £8.00			
	Hours spent on production	Hours worked on indirect work	Notes	Basic pay £	Overtime premium £	Total pay £
Monday	6	2	10am-12am cleaning of machinery	64	8	72
Tuesday	2	4	9am-1pm customer care course	48	0	48
Wednesday	8			64	8	72
Thursday	6			48	0	48
Friday	6	1	3-4pm health and safety training	56	4	60
Saturday	6			48	24	72
Sunday	3			0	48	48
Total	37	7		328	92	420

18   Employee's weekly timesheet for week ending 7 June

Employee: J Manford						
Employee number: P380				Basic pay per hour: £10.00		
	Hours spent on production	Hours worked on indirect work	Notes	Basic pay £	Overtime premium £	Total pay £
Monday	8	2	10am-12am Customer care training	100	5	105
Tuesday	4	2	9am-11am cleaning of equipment	60	0	60
Wednesday	10			100	5	105
Thursday	8			80	0	80
Friday	8	1	3-4pm health and safety training	90	2.50	92.50
Saturday	8			80	50	130
Sunday	4			0	80	80
Total	50	5		510	142.50	652.50

19   **Employee's weekly timesheet for week ending 31 January**

	Hours spent on production	Hours worked on indirect work	Notes	Basic pay £	Overtime premium £	Total pay £
Employee: Olivia Michael			**Profit Centre:** Moulding Department			
Employee number: P450			**Basic pay per hour:** £10.00			
Monday	5	3	10am-1pm cleaning moulds	80	2.50	82.50
Tuesday	3	4	9am-1pm fire training	70	0	70.00
Wednesday	8			80	2.50	82.50
Thursday	6	1		70	0	70.00
Friday	6	1	3-4pm annual appraisal	70	0	70.00
Saturday	3			30	7.50	37.50
Total	**31**	**9**		400	12.50	412.50

20 Employee's weekly timesheet for week ending 31 March

Employee: J. Webb				Profit Centre: Mixing department		
Employee number: P213				Basic pay per hour: £7		
	Hours spent on production	Hours worked on indirect work	Notes	Basic pay £	Overtime premium £	Total pay £
Monday	7			49	0	49
Tuesday	7	2	Weekly Staff meeting 1 hour	63	7	70
Wednesday	7	1		56	3.5	59.50
Thursday	5	2	Machine set up – 2 hrs	49	0	49
Friday	7			49	0	49
Saturday	3			21	0	21
Sunday	3		Stock taking	0	42	42
Total	39	5		287	52.50	339.50

Labour Bookkeeping

21

	Choice
Transaction 1	(A) Dr. Wages control, Cr. Bank
Transaction 2	(B) Dr. Work-in-progress, Cr. Wages control
Transaction 3	(C) Dr. Production overhead account, Cr. Wages Control
Transaction 4	(D) Dr. Production overhead control, Cr. Bank

ACCOUNTING FOR OVERHEADS

Overhead allocation and apportionment

22

	Basis of apportionment	Plastic moulding £000	Plastic extrusion £000	Maintenance £000	Stores £000	Canteen £000	Totals £000
Depreciation of plant and equipment	NBV of plant and equipment	7,500	15,000				22,500
Power for production machinery	Production machinery power usage (KwH)	7,500	10,000				17,500
Rent and rates	Floor space	4,750	4,750	2,375	7,125	4,750	23,750
Light and heat	Floor space	1,250	1,250	625	1,875	1,250	6,250
Indirect labour	Allocated			10,000	12,500	36,000	58,500
Totals		21,000	31,000	13,000	21,500	42,000	128,500
Reapportion Maintenance		10,400	2,600	(13,000)			
Reapportion Stores		10,750	10,750		(21,500)		
Reapportion Canteen		21,000	21,000			(42,000)	
Total overheads to production centres		63,150	65,350				128,500

23

	Basis of apportionment	Wood cutting £	Wood finishing £	Maintenance £	Stores £	General Admin £	Totals £
Depreciation of plant and equipment	NBV of plant and equipment	1,013,229	434,241				1,447,470
Power for production machinery	Production machinery power usage (KwH)	772,200	514,800				1,287,000
Rent and rates	Floor space			94,050	56,430	37,620	188,100
Light and heat	Floor space			20,790	12,474	8,316	41,580
Indirect labour	Allocated			182,070	64,890	432,180	679,140
Totals		1,785,429	949,041	296,910	133,794	478,116	3,643,290
Reapportion Maintenance		207,837	89,073	(296,910)			
Reapportion Stores		86,966	46,828		(133,794)		
Reapportion General Admin		239,058	239,058			(478,116)	
Total overheads to production centres		2,319,290	1,324,000				3,643,290

24

	Basis of apportionment	Assembly £	Finishing £	Maintenance £	Stores £	General Admin £	Totals £
Depreciation of plant and equipment	NBV of plant and equipment	420,000	280,000				700,000
Power for production machinery	Production machinery power usage (KwH)	403,000	217,000				620,000
Rent and rates	Floor space			48,000	32,000	20,000	100,000
Light and heat	Floor space			9,600	6,400	4,000	20,000
Indirect labour	Allocated			102,000	40,000	240,000	382,000
Totals		823,000	497,000	159,600	78,400	264,000	1,822,000
Reapportion Maintenance		119,700	39,900	(159,600)			
Reapportion Stores		39,200	39,200		(78,400)		
Reapportion General Admin		132,000	132,000			(264,000)	
Total overheads to production centres		1,113,900	708,100				1,822,000

25

	Basis of apportionment	Moulding £	Painting £	Maintenance £	Stores £	General Admin £	Totals £
Depreciation of plant and equipment	NBV of plant and equipment	238,627	297,833				
Power for production machinery	Production machinery power usage (KwH)	246,458	230,142				
Rent and rates	Floor space			42,743	14,564	12,348	69,655
Light and heat	Floor space			9,450	3,220	2,730	15,400
Indirect labour	Allocated			67,431	24,035	160,070	251,536
Totals		484,725	527,975	119,624	41,819	175,148	336,591
Reapportion Maintenance		89,718	29,906	(119,624)			
Reapportion Stores		16,728	25,091		(41,819)		
Reapportion General Admin		87,574	87,574			(175,148)	
Total overheads to production centres		678,745	670,546				1,349,291

26

	Basis of apportionment	Moulding £	Painting £	Maintenance £	Canteen £	General Admin £	Totals £
Depreciation of plant and equipment	NBV of plant and equipment	190,613	238,267				428,880
Power for production machinery	Production machinery power usage (KwH)	197,166	184,114				381,280
Rent and rates	Floor space			34,195	11,651	9,878	55,724
Light and heat	Floor space			7,560	2,576	2,184	12,320
Indirect labour	Allocated			53,945	19,228	128,056	201,229
Totals		387,779	422,381	95,700	33,455	140,118	1,079,433
Reapportion Maintenance		52,635	43,065	(95,700)			
Reapportion Canteen		20,909	12,546		(33,455)		
Reapportion General Admin		93,412	46,706			(140,118)	
Total overheads to production centres		554,735	524,698				1,079,433

Overhead absorption

27 (a) Plastic moulding = 22,500/15,000 = £1.50 and Plastic extrusion = 24,750/20,000 = £1.24 **The correct answer is A**

(b) Plastic moulding = 22,500/5,000 = £4.50 and Plastic extrusion = 24,750/5,200 = £4.76 **The correct answer is B**

(c) Plastic moulding = 22,500 – 19,800 = £2,700 over absorbed and Plastic extrusion = 24,750 – 38,000 = £13,250 under absorbed **The correct answer is B**

28 (a) Wood cutting = 586,792/9,464 = £62 and Wood finishing = 320,760/5,940 = £54 **The correct answer is D**

(b) Wood cutting = 586,792/29,340 = £20 and Wood finishing = 320,760/17,820 = £18 **The correct answer is A**

(c) Wood cutting = 586,792 – 568,631 = £18,161 over absorbed and Wood finishing = 320,760 – 356,580 = £35,820 under absorbed **The correct answer is B**

29 (a)   Assembly = 155,000/2,000 = £77.50 and Finishing = 105,000/1,750 = £12
         The correct answer is B

     (b)   Assembly = 155,000/12,500 = £12.40 and Finishing = 105,000/1,750 = £12
         The correct answer is D

     (c)   Assembly = 155,000 – 132,000 = £23,000 over absorbed and Finishing = 105,000 – 119,000 = £14,000 under absorbed **The correct answer is B**

30 (a)   Moulding = 36,000/18,000 = £2 and Painting = 39,000/1,200 = £32.50
         The correct answer is A

     (b)   Moulding = 36,000/9,000 = £4 and Painting = 39,000/13,000 = £3
         The correct answer is B

     (c)   Moulding = 36,000 – 37,500 = £1,500 under absorbed and Painting = 39,000 – 42,000 = 3,000 under absorbed **The correct answer is D**

31 (a)   Mixing = 64,800/10,000 = £6.48 and Bagging = 70,200/12,000 = £5.85
         The correct answer is A

     (b)   Mixing = 64,800/1,620 = £40 and Bagging = 70,200/2,340 = £30
         The correct answer is C

     (c)   Mixing = 64,800 – 67,500 = £2,700 under absorbed and Bagging = 70,200 – 75,600 = £5,400 under absorbed **The correct answer is B**

PROCESS COSTING

Losses

32

Description	Kg's	Unit cost £	Total cost £	Description	Kg's	Unit cost £	Total cost £
Material A	250	6	1,500	Normal loss	75	0.60	45
Material B	425	4	1,700	Output	675	14.34	9680
Material C	75	5	375				
Labour			2,400				
Overheads			3,750				
	750		9725		750		9725

	Debit	Credit
Abnormal loss		✓
Abnormal gain	✓	

33

Description	Kg's	Unit cost £	Total cost £	Description	Kg's	Unit cost £	Total cost £
Material TR10	1,080	2.16	2,333	Normal loss	126	1.08	136
Material DG41	720	2.70	1,944	Output	2,300	8.316	19,127
Material IG11	720	1.10	792	Abnormal loss	94	8.316	782
Labour			5,760				
Overheads			9,216				
	2,520		20,045		2,520		20,045

34 Process account

Description	Kg's	Unit cost £	Total cost £	Description	Kg's	Unit cost £	Total cost £
Material XG4	700	1.3	910	Normal loss	34	0.50	17
Material XH3	500	1.12	560	Output	1,600	4.93	7,888
Material XJ9	500	0.72	360	Abnormal loss	66	4.93	325
Labour			2,560				
Overheads			3,840				
	1,700		8,230		1,700		8,230

Normal loss account

Description	Kg's	Unit cost £	Total cost £	Description	Kg's	Unit cost £	Total cost £
Process account	34	0.5	17	Cash			50
Abnormal loss	66	0.5	33				
			50				50

Abnormal loss/gain account

Description	Kg's	Unit cost £	Total cost £	Description	Kg's	Unit cost £	Total cost £
Process account	66	4.93	325	Normal loss	66	0.50	33
				Profit and loss			292
			325				325

35

Description	Units	Unit cost £	Total cost £	Description	Units	Unit cost £	Total cost £
Input - Statues	300	11.25	3,375	Normal loss	30	5.00	150
Materials - Glaze			500	Output	290	49.35	14,312
Labour			5,760				
Overheads			3,840				
Abnormal gain	20	49.35	987				
Totals	320		14,462		320		14,462

36 (a)

Description	Litres	Cost per litre £	Total cost £	Description	Litres	Cost per litre £	Total cost £
Liquid X12	500	0.02	10	Normal loss	40	0.05	2
Liquid X13	200	0.04	8	Output	760	5.86	4,452
Liquid X14	100	0.10	10				
Labour			3,840				
Overheads			576				
Totals	800		4,454		800		4,454

(b)

	Debit	Credit
Abnormal loss		✓
Abnormal gain	✓	

Equivalent Units

37

Statement of EU

	Materials	Conversion
Completed	5,000	5,000
CWIP	600	300
TOTAL EU	5,600	5,300
Costs		
Period Costs	56,000	26,500
		10,600
TOTAL COSTS	56,000	37,100
Cost per EU	10.00	7.00

Description	Kgs	Total cost £		Description	Kgs	Total cost £
Materials	5,600	56,000		Completed	5,000	85,000
Labour		26,500		CWIP	600	8,100
Overheads		10,600				
	5,600	93,100			5,600	93,100

Workings:

Completed = 5,000 × (10 + 7) = £85,000

CWIP = 600 × 10 = 6,000

= 300 × 7 = 2,100

TOTAL = 8,100

38

Statement of EU

	Materials	Conversion
OWIP to complete	0	100
Completed output	2,950	2,950
CWIP	230	161
TOTAL EU	3,180	3,211
Costs		
Period Costs	135,000	99,000
TOTAL COSTS	42.4528	30.8315
Cost per EU		

Description	Units	Total cost £		Description	Units	Total cost £
OWIP	250	96,000		Completed	3,200	315,272
Materials	3,180	135,000		CWIP	230	14,728
Conversion		99,000				
	3,430	330,000			3,430	330,000

Working:

Completed = 100 × 30.8315 = 3,083
= 2,950× (42.4528 + 30.8315) = 212,189
+ OWIP b/f = 96,000
TOTAL = 315,272

CWIP = 230 × 42.4528 = 9764
= 161 × 30.8315 = 4964
TOTAL = 14,728

39

Equivalent units		Material	Conversion
	Completed Output	3,200	3,200
	CWIP	230	161
	Total EU	3,430	3,361
Costs			
	OWIP	54,000	42,000
	Period	135,000	99,000
	Total cost	189,000	141,000
Cost per EU		55.102	41.952

Description	Units	Total cost £		Description	Units	Total cost £
OWIP	250	96,000		Completed	3200	310,573
Materials	3,180	135,000		CWIP	230	19,427
Conversion		99,000				
		330,000				330,000

Working:

Completed = 3,200 × (55.102 + 41.952)   = 310,573

CWIP   = 230 × 55.102   =12,673
            = 161 × 41.952   = 6,754
                          TOTAL = 19,427

BASIC VARIANCE ANALYSIS

40

	Flexed Budget	Actual	Variance	Favourable F or Adverse A
Volume sold	18,500	18,500		
Sales revenue	37,000	38,850	1,850	F
Less costs:				
Direct materials	14,800	17,575	2,775	A
Direct labour	9,250	10,175	925	A
Overheads	2,000	1,950	50	F
Operating profit	10,950	9,150	1,800	A

41

	Flexed Budget	Actual	Variance	Favourable F or Adverse A.
Volume sold	259,200	259,200		
	£000	£000	£000	
Sales revenue	5,184	6,480	1,296	F
Less costs:				
Direct materials	907	954	47	A
Direct labour	1,037	864	173	F
Overheads	1,764	2,210	446	A
Operating profit	1,476	2,452	976	F

42

	Flexed Budget	Actual	Variance	Favourable F or Adverse A.
Volume sold	267,000	267,000		
	£000	£000	£000	
Sales revenue	2,136	2,409	273	F
Less costs:				
Direct materials	534	801	267	A
Direct labour	267	267	0	0
Overheads	600	750	150	A
Operating profit	735	591	144	A

43

	Flexed Budget	Actual	Variance	Favourable F or Adverse A
Volume sold	28,800	28800		
	£000	£000	£000	
Sales revenue	4,320	3,877	443	A
Less costs:				
Direct materials	252	212	40	F
Direct labour	1,260	912	348	F
Overheads	445	448	3	A
Operating profit	2,363	2,305	58	A

44

	Flexed Budget	Actual	Variance	Favourable F or Adverse A
Volume sold	5,000	5,000		
	£000	£000	£000	
Sales revenue	1,875	1,950	75	F
Less costs:				
Direct materials	45	45	0	0
Direct labour	220	182	38	F
Overheads	89	90	1	A
Operating profit	1,521	1,633	112	F

SHORT TERM DECISION MAKING

Cost Volume Profit analysis

45

(a) $\dfrac{9,952}{29-21} = 1,244$ units

(b) $\dfrac{9,952}{8/29} = £36,076$

Or $1,244 \times 29 = £36,076$

(c)

Units of GG99 sold	5,000	6,000
	£	£
Margin of safety (units)	$5,000 - 1,244 = 3,756$ units	$5,000 - 1,244 = 4,756$
Margin of safety percentage	$\dfrac{5,000 - 1,244}{5,000} \times 100 = 75.12\%$	$\dfrac{6,000 - 1,244}{6,000} \times 100 = 79.27\%$

(d) $\dfrac{9,952 + 48,000}{8} = 7,244$ units

(e) The correct answer is D – a reduction in selling price means that contribution per unit reduces therefore more units have to be made to cover the fixed costs. If BEP is higher then the margin of safety is lower.

46

(a) $\dfrac{64,800}{41.40 - 27} = 4,500$ units

(b) $\dfrac{64,800}{14.4/41.4} = £186,300$

Or $4,500 \times 41.4 = £186,300$

(c)

Units of MR 13 sold	9,000	10,800
	£	£
Margin of safety (units)	9,000 − 4,500 = 4,500 units	10,800 − 4,500 = 2,700 units
Margin of safety percentage	$\dfrac{9,000 - 4,500}{9,000} \times 100 = 50\%$	$\dfrac{10,800 - 4,500}{10,800} \times 100 = 58.33\%$

(d) $\dfrac{64,800 + 36,000}{14.4} = 7,000$ units

(e) The correct answer is A - an increase in selling price means that contribution per unit increases therefore less units have to be made to cover the fixed costs. If BEP is lower then the margin of safety is higher.

47

(a) $\dfrac{17,000}{19 - 12} = 2,429$ units

(b) $\dfrac{17,000}{7/19} = £46,142.86$

Or $2,429 \times 19 = £46,151$ (difference is due to rounding up the BEP units)

(c)

Units of CoralZ sold	4,000	5,000
	£	£
Margin of safety (units)	4,000 − 2,429 = 1,571 units	5,000 − 2,429 = 2,571 units
Margin of safety percentage	$\dfrac{4,000 - 2,429}{4,000} \times 100 = 39.28\%$	$\dfrac{5,000 - 2,429}{5,000} \times 100 = 51.42\%$

(d) $\dfrac{17,000 + 25,000}{7} = 6,000$ units

(e) The correct answer is B - an increase in selling price means that contribution per unit increases therefore less units have to be made to cover the fixed costs. If BEP is lower then the margin of safety is higher.

48

(a) $\dfrac{25,000}{10-6} = 6,250$ units

(b) $\dfrac{25,000}{4/10} = £62,500$

Or $6,250 \times 10 = £62,500$

(c)

Units of Blackbird sold	7,000	8,000
	£	£
Margin of safety (units)	$7,000 - 6,250 = 750$ units	$8,000 - 6,250 = 1,750$ units
Margin of safety percentage	$\dfrac{7,000 - 6,250}{7,000} \times 100 = 10.71\%$	$\dfrac{8,000 + 6,250}{8,000} \times 100 = 21.88\%$

(d) $\dfrac{25,000 + 35,000}{4} = 15,000$ units

(e) The correct answer is D - a reduction in selling price means that contribution per unit reduces therefore more units have to be made to cover the fixed costs. If BEP is higher then the margin of safety is lower.

49

(a) $\dfrac{15,000}{0.1 - 0.04} = 250,000$ units

(b) $\dfrac{15,000}{0.06/0.1} = £25,000$

Or $250,000 \times 0.1 = £25,000$

(c)

Units of Rose sold	300,000	400,000
	£	£
Margin of safety (units)	$300,000 - 250,000 = 50,000$ units	$400,000 - 250,000 = 150,000$ units
Margin of safety percentage	$\dfrac{300,000 - 250,000}{300,000} \times 100 = 16.67\%$	$\dfrac{400,000 - 250,000}{400,000} \times 100 = 37.5\%$

(d) $\dfrac{15,000 + 5,000}{0.06} = 333,334$ units

(e) The correct answer is C - an increase in selling price means that contribution per unit increases therefore less units have to be made to cover the fixed costs. If BEP is lower then the margin of safety is higher.

Limiting factor analysis

50

	Apple (£)	Banana (£)	Total (£)
Selling price per bar	3	2.40	
Less: variable costs per unit			
Direct materials	0.4	0.5	
Direct labour	0.24	0.28	
Variable overheads	0.3	0.38	
Contribution per unit	2.06	1.24	
Sales volume (bars)	75,000	125,000	
Total contribution	154,500	155,000	309,500
Less: fixed costs			150,000
Budgeted profit or loss			159,500

Product	Apple bars	Banana bars	Total
Contribution/unit (£)	2.06	1.24	
Machine hours/unit	0.4	0.16	
Contribution/machine hour (£)	5.15	7.75	
Product ranking	2	1	
Machine hours available			35,000
Machine hours allocated to: Product ..Banana.. Product ...Apple.	15,000	20,000	
Units made	37,500	125,000	
Total contribution	77,250	155,000	232,250
Less: fixed costs (£)			150,000
Profit/loss made (£)			82,250

51

	Squeaker (£)	Hooter (£)	Total (£)
Selling price per bar	1.25	1.75	
Less: variable costs per unit			
Direct materials	0.5	0.25	
Direct labour	0.25	0.5	
Variable overheads	0.25	0.65	
Contribution per unit	0.25	0.35	
Sales volume (units)	80,000	70,000	
Total contribution	20,000	24,500	44,500
Less: fixed costs			15,000
Budgeted profit			29,500

Product	Squeaker	Hooter	Total
Contribution/unit (£)	0.25	0.35	
Machine hours/unit	0.5	0.25	
Contribution/machine hour (£)	0.5	1.4	
Product ranking	2	1	
Machine hours available			50,000
Machine hours allocated to: Product ...Hooter Product ...Squeaker	32,500	17,500	
Units made	65,000	70,000	
Total contribution	16,250	24,500	40,750
Less: fixed costs (£)			15,000
Profit made (£)			25,750

LONG TERM DECISION MAKING

NPV and payback

52 (a)

	Year 0 £000	Year 1 £000	Year 2 £000	Year 3 £000
Capital expenditure	(450)			
Sales income		600	650	750
Operating costs		420	480	530
Net cash flows	(450)	180	170	220
PV factors	1.0000	0.8696	0.7561	0.6575
Discounted cash flows	(450)	157	129	145
Net present value	(19)			

The net present value is **negative**

(b)

Year	Cash flow £000	Cumulative cash flow £000
0	(450)	(450)
1	180	(270)
2	170	(100)
3	220	120

The payback period is **2** years and **6** months.

Months = 100/220 × 12 = 5.5 months

53 (a)

	Year 0 £000	Year 1 £000	Year 2 £000	Year 3 £000
Capital expenditure	(1,620)			
Sales income		756	1,008	1,440
Operating costs		216	270	342
Net cash flows	(1,620)	540	738	1,098
PV factors	1.0000	0.8696	0.7561	0.6575
Discounted cash flows	(1,620)	470	558	722
Net present value	130			

The net present value is **positive**

(b)

Year	Cash flow £000	Cumulative cash flow £000
0	(1,620)	(1,620)
1	540	(1,080)
2	738	(342)
3	1,098	756

The payback period is **2** years and **4** months.

Months = 342/1,098 × 12 = 3.7 months

54 (a)

	Year 0 £000	Year 1 £000	Year 2 £000	Year 3 £000
Capital expenditure	(1,200)			
Sales income		530	570	700
Operating costs		140	160	190
Net cash flows	(1,200)	390	410	510
PV factors	1.0000	0.8696	0.7561	0.6575
Discounted cash flows	(1,200)	339	310	335
Net present value	(216)			

The net present value is **negative**

(b)

Year	Cash flow £000	Cumulative cash flow £000
0	(1,200)	(1,200)
1	390	(810)
2	410	(400)
3	510	110
4	530	640

The payback period is **2** years and **9** months.

Months = 400/510 × 12 = 9.4 months

55 (a)

	Year 0 £000	Year 1 £000	Year 2 £000	Year 3 £000
Capital expenditure	(500)			
Sales income		280	330	390
Operating costs		100	120	130
Net cash flows	(500)	180	210	260
PV factors	1.0000	0.909	0.826	0.751
Discounted cash flows	(500)	164	173	195
Net present value	32			

The net present value is **positive**

(b)

Year	Cash flow £000	Cumulative cash flow £000
0	(500)	(500)
1	180	(320)
2	210	(110)
3	260	150

The payback period is **2** years and **5** months.

Months = 110/260 × 12 = 5.1 months

56 (a)

	Year 0 £000	Year 1 £000	Year 2 £000	Year 3 £000
Capital expenditure	(547)			
Sales income		290	340	400
Operating costs		(120)	(120)	(120)
Net cash flows	(547)	170	220	280
PV factors	1.0000	0.909	0.826	0.751
Discounted cash flows	(547)	155	182	210
Net present value	nil			

The net present value is **NIL**

(b)

Year	Cash flow £000	Cumulative cash flow £000
0	(547)	(547)
1	170	(377)
2	220	(157)
3	280	123

The payback period is **3** years and **7** months.

Months = 157/280 × 12 = 6.7 months.